IT'S NOT YOUR IQ, IT'S YOUR "I WILL"

TED D'ERAMO

God Bless
Ted

xulon PRESS

www.xulonpress.com

I am thankful for my wife, Lucetta, who encouraged me not to stop in this endeavor, assisted me with the book and helped me keep moving forward. I am grateful for our daughter, Erica, who has been on my side with countless hours to help and assist me to stay focus on this journey. I want to thank my granddaughter, Adrianna, for helping me. I am thankful for Scott Davis and Kendra Bergers who assisted with editing. I thank God for the Higher Ground Ministry and the life experiences I have encountered and the opportunity to continue to help others. A special thank you for Pastor Dave DeVries who preached, encouraged me and gave me the opportunity to start the Higher Ground Ministry.

Table of Contents

Introduction

It's Not Your IQ, It's Your "I Will"

It is not about how smart you are, how well you did in school, or the level of education you have that makes a person successful and productive. It is about your willingness to accept where you are in life and not quit. Your "I will" is your willingness to go after and achieve what is in front of you and not look back at your regrets and what you do not have. If you are willing, God will guide and equip you for this journey.

You don't have to be smart in order to change and have peace in your life. Change comes from seeing where you are, recognizing the need for change, and seeking help. This takes humility and the willingness to surrender.

This book is based on challenges and experiences that the author has lived and desires to share with others. With each "I will" there are suggestions to better your life in a positive way.

Chapter 1

I Will...Surrender

Can anyone change?

The answer to this question is very simple: Yes. Anyone can change. So why is it so difficult for us to change our lives? Most of us have been trying to change our lives for so long that we do not think there is any way to change.

Change can be difficult since it makes us feel uncomfortable. I remember someone telling me, "If you hold a baby and you smell something, you know what needs to be done. The baby needs to be changed." A baby is content and pleasant until you start to change his diaper and begins to cry. While the baby is in his mess, he feels happy, but as soon as you change the baby's environment, he cries until you have finished cleaning him up. Then he becomes content again. Isn't that just like us? We become content and even comfortable in the mess we have made in our lives.

As I look back at my past, I can remember my life was totally out of control. In my mind, I believed I was fine, and I felt like there was nothing wrong in how I was living. Part of it had to do with the people I surrounded myself with. I was living in a make-believe world, and I would stay at the billiard club playing pool all day long. However, I didn't care about my education or about making my life better. This was a way of escaping from my responsibilities. My friends and I used to hang around an old hotdog stand, and we would get in trouble. Sometimes we would fight, gamble and chase after girls. Now I know why the girls really didn't want to be around us. These actions made me feel comfortable, so I did not have to deal with my world.

Pride is another barrier that can keep us from changing. Pride can be a false belief that says, "I can deal with it later." Pastor Tony Gibson talks about pride on Page 20 in the Higher Ground Ministry Precept booklet. He writes: *"One who is proud has an inaccurate self-image. He thinks too highly of himself. The problem with many addicts is not low self-esteem but high self-esteem. They tend to overlook their faults and to accentuate their assets. Their pride gets in the way and dominates their lives."*

Humility is an important character quality for change to be successful. The opposite of being humble is being proud. A proud person may say, "I don't have a problem" or "I'm alright" even though his world is falling apart around him. Being proud blinds a person from seeing the truth of their situation and the harm it can cause others and even themselves. Proverbs 16:18 states, *"Pride goes before destruction, and a haughty spirit before a fall."* Therefore, we need to take an honest look at our situations and stop deceiving ourselves.

Feelings of fear and unworthiness can also limit our ability to change. For example, men and women who have been in jail for a long time may experience these feelings which can keep them from progressing into a better life.

I am a mason contractor, and after I was sober for one year, I did a job for a former police officer named Pete. One day, Pete invited me to go to church with him. I really did not want to go because I was scared, and I did not feel worthy of being in a church. I thought only "good people" went to church. How could I go there with all the wrong that I had done? I had been arrested at least 23 times that I can remember, and my addictive lifestyle brought me to federal prison. I made up an excuse because I felt unworthy and told Pete I could not go to church because I did not have any good clothes to wear. He told me not to worry because the church had an evening service and people dressed casually. Finally, I had no excuse.

The first time I went to the church, there was a time of sharing. In my mind, I wanted to see if these people were real or not. I stood up and said, "My name is Ted, and I am an alcoholic and drug addict. I'm not here for you, I'm here for God." Apparently God started to work in me because I continued to go to this church for a few months. I was surprised to see how the people welcomed and accepted me. I was able to go to church and not feel threatened or insecure.

Each week, I listened to the pastor share about Christ and invite people to accept Jesus as their Lord and Savior. One Sunday, at the end of his sermon, as always, he asked everyone in the church to close their eyes and put their heads down. So what did I do? I looked up to make sure everyone's heads were down. Then he asked, "Would anyone like to have Jesus in their life? If so, raise your hand." I had a struggle going on within myself, but I knew in this moment that nothing I tried to do ever worked, and I needed Jesus to change my life. So I released my pride and fear, and I surrendered by raising my hand to receive Christ.

Then the pastor asked everyone to stand up, and the church sang a hymn and invited everyone who raised their hands to come forward. I knew the pastor saw me raise my hand, and I went forward. I was led into a room with a few church leaders who shared a Bible verse about faith with me. The verse is found in Matthew 17:20 and says, *"...Truly I tell you, if you have faith as small as a mustard seed, you can say to this mountain, 'Move from here to there,' and it will move. Nothing will be impossible for you."* In Mark 4:31-32, we learn about the actual size of the mustard seed. The verse says, *"It is like a mustard seed, which is the smallest of all seeds on earth. Yet when planted, it grows and becomes the largest of all the garden plants, with such big branches that the birds can perch in its shade."*

Surrendering to Christ is a key action to achieving a changed life. I may not have had a lot of faith, but I did have that "mustard seed faith," and my life has never been the same since.

EDITOR NOTE
Quote by Dr. A. L. Gibson, 2007. "Precepts"

Chapter 2

I Will...Not Give Up

How long does it take to change?

There is no easy answer to this question because everyone is different. Think of some people you know who find it challenging to make personal changes. Do you see patterns in their lives that keep them from changing? Many people have fear or pride that keeps them from changing their ways. They can make excuses, or they blame others for their problems, or they may think they are not as bad as other people. This ultimately is an issue of avoidance to finding solutions. Change takes longer when the problems get denied and excuses are made.

Now think of the people you know whose lives have changed. Can you see the difference in their lives? I know people who have surrendered their lives to God and never went back to their former ways of living. God can change you and make you into a new creation. In the Bible, the apostle Paul shares with us in 2

Corinthians 5:17, *"Therefore, if anyone is in Christ, he is a new creation; old things have passed away; behold, all things have become new"* (NKJV).

A good way of looking at change is understanding that is a process. First, you must get serious. Make a decision to change and stick to it. Your willingness to fully commit to changing plays a very important role in this process and the outcomes.

Secondly, it is important to look at the people in your life. Consider if they are hurting you or if they pull you in the wrong direction. In 1 Corinthians 15:33, we are warned about the people we spend our time with. The verse states, *"Do not be misled: bad company corrupts good character."* The people you associate with carry a big influence on what you do, how you think, and the way you live your life. Sometimes people live like chameleons that change the color of their skin to blend in and camouflage with their environment. An example of this is if you hang around with swimmers and you never swim, eventually, you will start to swim. Why? Because there is this desire to be accepted.

In my life, this is how my addiction to heroin began. I hated needles, but the people I spent my time with were using heroin. They began to help me with the needles to inject heroin. From my experiences, most drug users make sure they have enough drugs for the day. Once I became able to use heroin by myself, I helped others who wanted to get high and were afraid of injecting themselves. I was willing to help them so I would get some of their heroin. This became a vicious cycle. I not only hurt myself, but I helped others to do the same. You are the only one who is responsible for who you choose to spend your time with. How you spend your time with your friends can dramatically affect how you live each day.

I know people who have experienced moments of change in their lives because they faced challenges. Relationships with their family, spouse, and children were being destroyed. Others had pressure from their jobs because of poor performance, and some people had been involved with the court system. These people may have been able to change their lives for a while and life improved in the short term. But once the pressure came off and challenges diminished, they reverted back to their former ways.

Jesus told a story which explains this well. It is the parable about the four soils found in Matthew 13:3b-9.

Then he told them many things in parables, saying: "A farmer went out to sow his seed. As he was scattering the seed, (1) some fell along the path, and the birds came and ate it up. (2) Some fell on rocky places, where it did not have much soil. It sprang up quickly, because the soil was shallow. But when the sun came up, the plants were scorched, and they withered because they had no root. (3) Other seed fell among thorns, which grew up and choked the plants. (4) Still other seed fell on good soil, where it pro-duced a crop—a hundred, sixty or thirty times what was sown. He who has ears let him hear."

In Matthew 13:18-23, Jesus explains the significance of this parable.

> *"Listen to what the parable of the sower means: (1) When anyone hears the message about the kingdom and does not understand it, the evil one comes and snatches away what was sown in their heart. This is the seed sown along the path. (2) The seed falling on rocky ground refers to someone who hears the word and at once receives with joy. But since they have no root, they last only a short time. When trouble or persecution comes because of the word, he quickly falls away. (3) The seed falling among the thorns refers to someone who hears the word, but the worries of this life and the deceitfulness of wealth choke the word, making it unfruitful. (4) But the seed falling on good soil refers to someone who hears the word and understands it. This is the one who produces a crop, yielding a hundred, sixty or thirty times what was sown."*

Which "soil" best describes you? Have lies and your sins kept you from knowing God? Has your faith in Christ been uprooted due to troubles in this world? Is your life being choked by wealth or worries of this life? Or do you have a faith that is secure and evident in your life?

The Israelites are an example to us of how unwillingness to surrender to God has consequences. Their journey to the Promised Land could have taken only 11 days per the account in Deuteronomy 1:2. Yet, because of their stubbornness, complacency, and disobedience, they wandered and complained in the wilderness for 40 years. A whole generation did not even see or enter the Promised Land. Aren't we often like the Israelites? We want our lives to change, but we keep getting in the way of God's plans for us.

Another problem many people face is that they become complacent and comfortable. They feel good because they have a nice car, family, money, and material possessions. Change becomes harder when we get distracted from these possessions and keeps us from getting closer to God. I believe that God wants us to love Him first and He will give us the desires of our hearts, according to His will. Psalm 37:4 says, *"Delight yourself in the LORD and He will give you the desires of your heart"* (NASB).

So, put God first and expect the blessings. I don't know if the blessings will be health, finances, or peace within; but I do know God wants us to put Him first before all other things.

Recently I received a phone call about a man I met while he was in a program. This program allowed me to bring men to Higher Ground meetings and to church services regularly. I think it had been two years since I last heard from him. The phone call came at 12 o'clock one night from his girlfriend, asking me to help him. She was pleading for help. So I said, "Let me talk to him." She told me he crashed his truck and was in bed. I told her to have him call me and please do not call me at midnight.

First of all, he did not call me for help. He was in bed or passed out from using drugs. Often we want people to do for us what only we can do for ourselves. If he really wanted help, he would have made the phone call. I do not know how long it will take for his situation to change. If he wants to change, he needs to get honest about his problems. If you desire to change, you need to be honest also.

Sometimes, when I help other people, I tell them that their best thinking got them to where they are today. It is not easy to do but why not let your best thinking get out of the way? Remember pride can be a hindrance for us to experience change but humility brings results.

The real question is not *how long does it take to change?* but rather *how badly do you want to change?* This is a question that needs to be taken seriously. If you are willing to get honest with yourself and seek help, you will be a step closer to a newer and more productive life.

Chapter 3

I Will...Look For the Winners

Do I have to change my friends?

M any times, we believe the friends we have are the best that can be expected. We often think our friends are not that bad and hope they will have a true desire to change their ways of living as well. However, most of the time, our friends, or so-called friends, do not want to change. This should be a warning sign in our relationships because their behaviors often impact how we live.

When you begin to change your life, your friends may begin to think that there is something wrong with you because you are not doing what you formerly did, such as getting high or drinking excessively. This may cause some confusion as to which way of living is right and which is wrong. I learned that I am not able to change anyone but myself. My friends have to come to the realization they need to change their lives also.

When I began to change, I came to the place of surrender in my life to begin my journey of recovery. I could no longer pretend that everything was okay in my life. I was on the methadone program that helps people trying to get off heroin. The social worker must have seen something in me because I was offered counseling and so my wife and I agreed to go. I remember at one of our sessions Nate, our counselor, said that he could not work with me unless I stopped drinking.

I went for help at this point of my life because of my heroin addiction, but I did not think I had a drinking problem. I sought help at an Alcoholics Anonymous (AA) support group. One of the first things I was told was to take a look at my friends. I was asked if any of my friends had been calling me since I was no longer getting high. For me, the answer was "no". When I stopped doing drugs and alcohol, they stopped calling me.

When you are in the process of changing your life, you become different than those who you were hanging out with. You will look at things differently, act differently, live differently, and think differently. The best way to develop new friendships is to find people who share your new values, Christian beliefs, and lifestyle.

When you make a decision to separate yourself from people who are influencing you negatively, remember to stand strong. Stay with your newly found friends, or as I like to say, "Stay with the winners." These are people who have been through tough times and have changed. I learned to spend time with the winners by attending meetings and church. God put people in my life who were able to help me. I challenge you to spend some time and look for the winners. Look for people who have qualities that you want to have in your life. Ask God to put people in your life who can help you on your road to recovery and relationship with God.

Years ago, as a small mason contractor, it was easy to just shake hands with the customer, and when the job was finished I was paid for the work I did. As time went on, my jobs began to get bigger in size and price. I started to deal with a different clientele who expected a written and signed contract. It was my responsibility for both parties to have a signed contract which explained what the job entailed and how I wanted to get paid.

My work continued to grow with larger jobs that had more responsibility and demands placed upon me. I was given a blueprint, and I would price the job according to what was on the blueprint. I was also given a spec book with 50 or more pages that specified the required materials that the client wanted used on the job as well as the details of the payments that we agreed upon. Sometimes I would go to business meetings to hear the progress of all the other contractors involved in their jobs and we shared how our work responsibilities and jobs were progressing. We would discuss how to keep our jobs on schedule with the various weather conditions and problems that we encountered.

As in business, situations happen in our everyday lives. I tell people that it is best to stop when you are comfortable. You don't have to do what the next guy is doing. I believe that this is true for our friendships. There may be many people who want to be your friend, but it is wise to take baby steps and not rush into relationships with every person who wants to be your friend. Get to know them well to see who they really are. Remember, God is willing and able to help you; all you need to do is ask for His wisdom and He will guide you. A good Bible verse to consider is Proverbs 3:5-6, *"Trust in the Lord with all your heart and do not lean on your own understanding. In all your ways acknowledge Him, and He will make your paths straight"* (NASB).

The Merriam-Webster Dictionary defines a "friend" as *"a person who you like and enjoy being with; a person who helps or supports someone or something (such as a cause or charity)."* These are two characteristics that we should consider as we form our friendships. People you enjoy spending time with and who will give you moral support and understanding needed in order to help you grow.

I have had a lot of people in my life that wanted to be my friend. Sometimes there was a conflict because the relationship was being built on what they wanted me to become or belong to. Let me give you an example. I met a man who became a friend. He was in a program, and we would go to Higher Ground meetings and church together. Sometimes we would eat together, and we talked frequently. The conflict began when he decided to start hanging around with bad company. His morals changed and were not the same as mine. I needed to separate myself from him in order to keep myself focused. Spending more time with him could influence me to make bad choices.

Another example of a conflict is if your new friend has a hobby that you are not interested in. Suppose your friend enjoys fishing and goes fishing three or more times a week. Here is where the problem shows up. If you don't like fishing, or like getting up early in the morning, or you get seasick, you might say to your friend, "I do not like fishing." This could cause a problem with the friendship because there is no common interest.

My suggestion about friendship is to find people who have a similar lifestyle and positive interests you like to do. This would make your friendship easier and more enjoyable.

Chapter 4

I Will...Find the Purpose

What will I do with myself?

As people begin to change their lives, there may be concerns, and a common question is: "What will I do with myself now that I'm not getting high or hanging around with my old friends?" I know I was living in a self-centered world. My life consisted of meeting up with my friends, and we would see who had the best drugs. Then we would go and try to buy some more drugs. Each day we would do the same thing. My life was pretty predictable. During this time of my life, I was living in a small world. Life was all about me as if I were the only one living in this world.

I was getting high for so many years that I began to think that doing drugs was the only way to live. But that is a lie. There are programs available today that were able to help me and can also help you. When I decided to attend AA, I realized stepping out for help was scary. I experienced moments of anxiety when I was in a new and unfamiliar situation with people I did not know. I remember the group leader asked me to make coffee before the meetings began. I said to myself, *"How can I do this? What if I mess up?"* but when you are willing to change, you need to step out.

One day, I was playing golf with a friend and we almost ran over a turtle with our golf cart, but the turtle went into its shell for safety. This reminded me of what one of my mentors told me, "A turtle cannot move unless it sticks its neck out." I stuck my neck out by facing my fear of messing up and committed to making the coffee for the AA meetings.

I can still remember the first time I made the coffee. Some of the old-timers came in early, like they normally did, and wanted to drink coffee before the meeting began. I thought I did a good job making the coffee, and I was so proud of myself. However, when the first person went to get a cup of coffee, what they poured was only hot water. I forgot to put the coffee grinds in the pot. This may seem like a silly story and not a big deal, but back then it was not too funny for me because I felt like I had failed and that was what I was afraid of. God must have a sense of humor because instead of taking away my coffee commitment, they asked me to commit for 6 months. God has a way of helping us when we step outside our comfort zone.

I also began sharing and participating at the AA meetings. Then there was a day when I was done with my coffee commitment. I felt pretty good about showing the next guy how to make the coffee. I began to feel better and started teaching people the things that I was learning. I think it is that simple. Go and teach someone or help someone else to move on in their life today.

When I began to change, I wondered what I was going to do with my life, and this was scary for me. I remember times when I would try to not get high, and I was faced with the feeling of loneliness. I felt like the world had changed and I was left all alone. Yet, in reality, I had changed. I could have been in a room with 100 people yet still I felt like I was all alone.

In those moments of feeling lonely, I had a choice to make. I could go back to my old ways of living, or I could deal with my feelings and emotions and grow into this new life. Besides loneliness, addressing my fears played a big role in my recovery. I had to remember that I was dealing with new feelings, and that feelings do not always tell the truth. Feelings are not facts and can change at any time in our lives.

When I got caught up in my lifestyle of sin, I thought that chasing drugs was fulfilling. However, it actually was a chore and never did truly satisfy me. My passion for drugs left me with hurt, guilt and remorse. The Merriam-Webster Dictionary defines "passion" as "*a strong feeling of enthusiasm or excitement for something or about doing something; a strong feeling such as anger that causes you to act in a dangerous way."* You can have a passion to sin or a passion to live for God. I want to challenge you to choose to be passionate about living for God, which reaps benefits for this life and eternity. Colossians 3:23-24 says, *"And whatever you do, do it heartily, as to the Lord and not to men, knowing that from the Lord you will receive the reward of the inheritance; for you serve the Lord Christ" (NKJV).*

One of the things I really enjoy doing is playing golf. For you, there may be another hobby or activity that you enjoy. I have attended church since 1978, and church is still a big part of my life. I enjoy spending time with my wife, family and God. These are things that I used to think seemed boring, but now I know that they are blessings and fun. I really like helping other people who are in the same place as I was and spending time with them as I help to guide them through their lives to a place of victory.

For me, I feel grateful as I see how God is using me in this area. I am now passionate about many good things. When you enjoy something it is not a chore, it can be fun and fulfilling. 1 John 5:3-4 says, *"In fact, this is love for God: to keep his commands. And his commands are not burdensome, for everyone born of God overcomes the world. This is the victory that has overcome the world, even our faith."* My relationship with God has given me the most satisfaction and purpose in my life.

Helping people turned out to be a passion in my life which is a gift from God. A gift is something that is given to you; it is not earned. God has blessed my life through this passion, and it is a joy to see other people come out of the slavery of addiction. My "small world" mentality has been lifted and I am no longer trying to live for myself. I now find more pleasure in serving God and others. To find your passion, try helping others by serving in the church or in the community, and you will discover what you are passionate about doing.

One night, I received a phone call from a man who was struggling with his life but finally surrendered to God. He came to me through a program, and I could see how excited he was to tell me how he prayed and accepted Jesus Christ as his Lord and Savior. The man who prayed with him thought he would never be able to tell someone about Jesus, but now he is passionate about helping others. This is an example of how I get blessed by others who are able to help other people.

We are all passionate about something. I once heard a pastor say, "If you want to know what you are passionate about, give me your checkbook and appointment book and the condition of your Bible, and I'll tell you from these three things where your passion is." What you give to or care about is an indication of what you are most passionate about. God has a purpose for your life so stick your neck out and trust Him.

Chapter 5

I Will...Make God First in My Life

When do I look for God in my life?

I searched everywhere for peace, and the last place I sought for peace was God. If you are wise, make God first in your lives. Yet, throughout the pages of the Bible, we find examples of how Adam and Eve faced consequences for disobeying God. We each face a choice of doing good or bad. Before sin entered Adam and Eve's lives, they lived wonderful lives without any pain or suffering in the Garden of Eden. God instructed them that they could eat from any tree and plant except from The Tree of The Knowledge of Good and Evil. Yet what did they choose? They listened to the lies from the devil and chose to eat from the tree that God commanded them not to eat from. Their disobedience led them to sin against God. Try to make time to read the whole story from Genesis 1 and 2 in the Bible.

We don't always know right from wrong. When a life-controlling habit controls one's thinking, they will justify their wrong behavior. This keeps the person in sinful patterns and behaviors which fulfills the definition of insanity. Insanity is doing the same things and expecting different results. Some people look to their parents for help in making choices. If their parents follow God, the chances are they will have less pain and sin in their lives. It is much easier to follow God, yet children may not have parents who have faith or people in their lives with strong moral convictions or values. As children get older, they start making choices that they think are good for themselves. Some choices may be good while others are actually unhealthy choices. Many people that I know have heard of God in the past yet rejected Him and decided to live in their own way. In my life, I chose drugs, heroin and alcohol.

I remember the first time I wanted to drink. I was 13 years old, and I did not know how to get alcohol. So I asked someone to help me buy a bottle of booze. I told him I would buy one for him if he got one for me. In reality, I did not know who this person was and really did not care. This person did not stop me and he never said to me that drinking was wrong. He was already in a place of not caring. I didn't think I would become like him and thought that alcohol was the answer to finding peace. Alcohol gave me a false sense of security and courage while allowing me to feel comfortable around people. I was able to talk with anyone about many things. This sense of security and peace was temporary and did not endure.

When I surrendered my life to Christ, I found lasting peace. It took me 32 years to find God, and I wish I found Him sooner. This would have saved me from making so many mistakes and having so many regrets in my life. I thank God that I am able to share the mistakes I have made in order to help other people learn not to make the same mistakes I did.

The sooner we take responsibility for our choices, the easier our lives will become. Our lives will become less crazy and a sense of sanity can return to our lives. I tell people that I did not quit, but I surrendered. It was easier to stop getting high than it was to get high. I realized that my body was falling apart and was not functioning well. I began to have grand mal seizures, and the seizures intensified the more I got high.

I know today that it takes a bigger person to say, "I'm done and I need help." When you get to that place in your life, don't waste your time on trying to do it your own way. Take a look at how your ways of thinking got you to where you are today. Don't be afraid of changing your life and seeking help from others.

I remember talking with my pastor, who could not relate to my past, but he had a way of talking to me that made me feel very comfortable. He made me feel loved and accepted. Life makes sense when we look at our past and accept the facts as they are. No matter how good or bad a person you are, God loves you and wants to be in your life. When we become Christians, God takes away our stony hearts and gives us new hearts. God tells us in Ezekiel 36:26, *"I will give you a new heart and put a new spirit in you. I will remove from you your heart of stone and give you a new heart of flesh."*

God forgives us and cleanses us because Jesus Christ died on the cross so our sins could be forgiven. In 1 John 1:9 the Bible teaches us that *"If we confess our sins, He is faithful and just and will forgive us our sins and purify us from all unrighteousness."* This is the grace of God.

My challenge to you is in the form of a question: What is stopping you from allowing God to be in your life? This is a question only you can answer. Please take the time to think about why God is not first in your life.

Chapter 6

I Will...Take the First Step

Is it important to have God in my life?

I know that surrendering to God was the last place that I turned for help. I tried almost everything out there from alcohol, cough medicine, heroin, marijuana, cocaine, speed, barbiturates, gambling and women. I was searching for peace in the things that the world offers. Yet, I have learned that none of them have ever compared with the peace that I have found in Jesus Christ. 1 John 2:15-17 teaches, *"Do not love the world or anything in the world. If anyone loves the world, the love of the Father is not in him. For everything in the world – the cravings of sinful man, the lust of his eyes and the boasting of what he has and does – comes not from the Father but from the world. The world and its desires pass away, but the man who does the will of God lives forever."*

I have learned the importance of having God in my life. I knew deep down inside that my actions did not give me peace, but actually left me in slavery and bondage to sin.

When someone introduced me to God years ago I first thought, "Here is another scam." I thought that there had to be something in it for them. There is a story told about W.C. Fields when he was in the hospital and was caught reading the Bible by his wife. He told her, "I am trying to look for the loopholes." I tried to find the loopholes in God because I needed to know if God was real for myself.

I had faith that was small, like a mustard seed; therefore, I became hungrier for more of God in my life. There was a new purpose placed within my heart. I could not get enough of God, His believers, and His teachings. I had a desire to learn more about God through His Word, and for opportunities to serve Him more. I attended prayer meetings, Bible studies and church services regularly.

As I continued to grow in my faith with God, I became more involved with different ministries and held leadership positions in my church. I discovered who the winners were and watched them live their lives in a better way. I watched how they responded to challenging situations in their lives. They had strong faith, and I longed for that same faith.

I learned that not only is it important to have God in my life, but it is equally important for me to follow Him as best as I can. I know I will face troubles in my life, but I am thankful that I know that God says, *"Never will I leave you; never will I forsake you"* (Hebrews 12:5).

I have seen how God has changed me from a selfish and self-centered person to a person who now cares for others and is living with peace. Before this change happened in my life, it was all about me. Now I truly want to help others experience the peace that only God can bring about. He took me out of the darkness and brought me into the light.

> *"But you are a chosen people, a royal priesthood, a holy nation, God's special possession, that you may declare the praises of him who called you out of darkness into his wonderful light."* 1 Peter 2:9

My life has taken on a new meaning and purpose. It became more important for me to try to help other people to change. Ultimately, it is God who changes a person but we can be used by Him through our testimonies and victories. If people remember how I used to be and see who I am today, they may be encouraged to change. I have discovered that it is a very good feeling and reassurance to know that God will use me wherever I am today to help make the lives of other people better. It does not matter where you are in life, but it does matter where you are going.

There have been many people who have asked me, "How do I begin a walk with God?" Someone once stated, "A journey of 1000 miles started with the first step." That first step is to surrender to God and to allow Him to be the Lord of your life. Do not let fear or anything in this world keep you from taking that all important first step so that you can receive the free gift of salvation that only Jesus can offer for anyone who asks for it.

> *If you declare with your mouth, "Jesus is Lord," and believe in your heart that God*

raised him from the dead, you will be saved.
Romans 10:9

Jesus did not go to Calvary's cross because He had nothing else to do. He died on the cross for people like you and me so that we can have eternal life and be forgiven of our sins. He knew that there was only one way to set us free. Jesus says in John 14:6, *"I am the way, and the truth and the life. No one comes to the Father except through me."*

Jesus Christ took on our sins. In other words, Jesus paid a debt that He never owed because we had a debt that we could never pay back. You cannot earn your way back to God. It is only experienced through grace. Grace has been described as "God's riches at Christ's expense." It is also characterized as "underserved favor." Ephesians 2:8-10 tells us, *"For it is by grace you have been saved, through faith–and this not from yourselves, it is the gift of God–not by works, so that no one can boast. For we are God's handiwork, created in Christ Jesus to do good works, which God prepared in advance for us to do."*

It is important to remember that your life is not an accident. Even though someone may have spoken that over you it is not true. Psalm 139:13-14 says, *"For you created my inmost being; you knit me together in my mother's womb. I praise you because I am fearfully and wonderfully made; your works are wonderful, I know that full well."*

My prayer for you is that you will find the peace that comes from taking your first step and surrendering your life to Christ. Once God is in your heart, you will begin to see life in a whole new and different way.

Chapter 7

I Will...Embrace Change

Can God change me?

God can and is willing to change us, but He is waiting for us to come to Him. Many people do not really know who God is or if God is real. As a child, I learned very little about my Catholic heritage and even less about who God was. Going to church was not important to my parents, so we did not normally attend. My parents were not the best role models for me because of their own personal problems; however, I do believe they did the best for me that they could. There was always food on the table and a roof over our heads, but learning about God was not a priority in our family.

I remember hearing about President Richard Nixon and the Watergate scandal. President Nixon had some of the most powerful men working under him. Yet being in a powerful position did not keep them from facing the fruit of their wrongdoings as being a part of this scandal. President Nixon was impeached, and many others resigned from their jobs or even went to jail as a result. I am sharing this to illustrate how people create problems for themselves because of their wrongdoings. These politicians acted as if they were above the law, yet their "power" did not keep them from their fall.

Now, when I think about God and His Son, Jesus Christ, I realize that He had no power according to the world's standards. He was born in a manger, worked as a carpenter, and yet it is through Him that sinners can be set free from the sins that keep them captive and enable them to have an abundant life now and for eternity.

Jesus lived His life as a servant as He taught crowds of people and individuals about what it means to be a follower of Christ. The Bible is the answer to any need we may be experiencing. As we read the Bible, we are able to understand God's truths and how to apply them to our lives. Jesus was full of love, and it is by His love that people would have salvation and forgiveness of sins. He demonstrated His compassion as He healed the sick, raised the dead and performed miracles. Matthew 9:35-36 states, *"Jesus went through all the towns and villages, teaching in their synagogues, proclaiming the good news of the kingdom and healing every disease and sickness. When he saw the crowds, he had compassion on them, because they were harassed and helpless, like sheep without a shepherd."*

My wife and I have experienced God's grace and His compassion in our own lives especially when we first became believers. We believed, and still do today, that God, Jesus Christ, and the Holy Spirit exist. We knew that we needed to have more of Him in our lives. As we sought a deeper and committed relationship with God, our lives began to change for the better. As a result, we attended Bible studies, church services, prayer meetings, and had a growing desire to know more of the Truth. In the past, we were slaves to our sins, but God opened our eyes and by His grace we have peace, purpose, and a desire to help others learn more about God and His amazing grace. We have discovered that God has changed our hearts to no longer desire our former unwholesome attitudes and false beliefs. Our dependence on God has grown into a deeper trust and faith in Him. Depending on God has truly changed our lives; we never imagined how good our lives would become.

All good relationships require nurturing, spending time together, communicating, listening and a desire to please the other person. Therefore, God is pleased when He knows that someone desires a relationship with Him. As we seek God by praying and talking to Him about our concerns and as we read the Bible and have fellowship with other believers, we will know more about God and how we are to live.

It doesn't matter how many bad influences you had in your life or your status of power and success in this world. What truly brings joy, contentment, satisfaction and value to life is a relationship with God.

God will provide a clear way and path for you to change as you trust in Him. Sometimes, this may not be easy because we often want to see the positive results immediately without putting a degree of effort into it. The process of changing your life is active. You have choices to make each and every day. Some choices are good and will take you a step closer to the positive change you want. However, there are other choices which are bad and will slow down your changing or even take you steps backwards.

Please don't be afraid to try God as I have along with countless of millions of others through the ages. All I can tell you is that I know I have peace in my life that I never had before. This peace is because I allowed God to change me.

He is the Potter and I am His clay. The more I allow Him in my life, the more easily it is for Him to mold me. Isaiah 64:8 says, "*Yet you, Lord, are our Father. We are the clay, you are the potter; we are all the work of your hand.*"

When Jesus started His ministry, He did not choose men who had it all together. His disciples were ordinary men from all walks of life. Peter was a fisherman, Matthew the tax collector, Simon the Zealot, and the list goes on. These men were all different but have one thing in common. They were willing to leave what they were doing to follow Jesus. Remember, "God does not call the qualified, He qualifies the called."

Jesus picked ordinary people like you and I to do some of the most extraordinary things. So, if their lives could change, why can't yours as well? I have seen many people surrender their lives to God. Once their lives were all about themselves, but as they surrendered, their focus changed. It happened because they changed from the inside out. Only God can do this, for He is a miracle worker. God changed me, and I know and believe that He can change you, too.

Chapter 8

I Will...Begin a Relationship with God

How do I begin this walk with God?

M any people feel that they are unworthy to have a relationship with God. They may not be completely ready to change and start a walk with Him. Let me encourage you by saying that none of us are really able to live up to God's standards; so, please do not let this stop you. Remember this Bible verse in Romans 3:23 which says, *"For all have sinned and fall short of the glory of God."* Don't worry about your image, how you appear before others, and what you need to do for God. We can come to God because He loves us.

As I mentioned previously, "a journey of 1000 miles starts with the first step." The beginning of your life with Christ is to pray and ask Jesus to come into your heart. If you don't know what to pray for or have never prayed, it is simply talking with God. I encourage you to find people who believe and are following Jesus Christ and ask them to pray with you. Remember that salvation is God's gift to us. What we do with it is our gift back to God.

"For it is by grace you have been saved, through faith—and this is not from yourselves, it is the gift of God—not by works, so that no one can boast." Ephesians 2:8-9

For me, when I felt like I had nowhere to go and nothing else worked, I gave my will over to God and asked Jesus to come into my heart. A change was happening in my mind and heart as this new way of living as a Christian made me feel good and was exciting for me. Before Christ, I thought I was okay with how I lived and treated other people around me but God began to show me the ways I was living and what I was doing that was not okay. I began to feel bad about how I was acting. I would feel uncomfortable and guilty for what I was doing and for what I did in the past. The Holy Spirit was convicting me and teaching me a different way to live. The way God wanted me to live. God is gentle and will reveal to us the things He wants us to change when we are ready and willing to change. Remember to listen for that small voice within you that wants to bring good changes into your life.

I met a guy who asked me a question: "How can I accept Jesus into my heart?" The next day, I saw him again and he asked me for a jump start on his car battery. I felt a burden that I needed to pray with him and I didn't want to miss this opportunity. As he put the cables on the battery, I told him to "wait a second, I want to talk with you." I began talking to him about Jesus, and he prayed to ask Jesus into his heart. This is one of the ways God orchestrated opportunities for me to witness in my life.

Another time, I was on Interstate 95 when I saw a woman on the side of the road who looked like she was having car problems. I pulled over and asked if I could help. She said she ran out of gas. I told her I would get some gas and be right back. I put the gas in the car, and she was ready to travel again. Before she was going to leave, she asked me how much she owed me. I asked her if she went to church. She said not right now. I said to her, "if you come to church on Sunday that would be more than enough for me." A couple weeks went by, and then her and her family were in church. They are now active in the church where they are serving God and enjoying their life with Him.

These are a couple of examples of how I have seen people's lives change when they were willing to give God a chance. If you are in a relationship with someone, the more time you spend together the more you grow closer and know each other better. Just like in relationships with others it takes a commitment, and the same goes for a relationship with God. The closer I became to God, the more I was able to discern the small voice within me, the Holy Spirit's nudges that allowed me to help someone or convicted me of my behavior. Wherever you are, it is a good place to start a relationship with God.

Chapter 9

I Will...Lead Others

How do I lead people?

I tell people that you have to know something before you can teach others something. I am now a retired mason contractor, but when I was younger, my father noticed that I was getting into trouble and not doing well in school. So he gave me a couple of choices. He said to me, "Either you go to school or you get a job." I decided to take what I thought was the easier road and I quit school after two months in the 9th grade. My father was a mason contractor, and as I was growing up, I saw that his business was successful. So with my great thinking, I went to work for him.

When I began to work, I wanted to start laying stone because we made many stone walls, but my dad told me that I first needed to learn how to mix cement. So one of his men started to teach me, and I learned quickly. The next thing I needed to do was to ensure that the masons had enough cement and stone so that they could continue working. Then I was able to install stone on the back side of the wall which is about 18 inches thick. By this time, I knew how to mix cement, how to prepare the material for the other workers, and how to build the back side of the wall. The masons would stop by and inspect how I was doing and offer suggestions as I progressed along in my trade. After learning these skills, I finally had the opportunity to lay stone on the front side of the wall. I still needed to learn from others and gain experience.

Remember that you cannot lead others until you have the knowledge or experience in what you are trying to teach them. I believe this not only pertains to business but also for discipleship and leading others in their relationship with God. Discipleship is an important commitment where you are involved in a persons' life for a period of time in order to teach them.

Through the Higher Ground Ministry I am able to build relationships with those who attend the meetings. I can help them because my life has changed and I am able to share what has helped me and about the importance of having a relationship with God. I invite them to attend church and Bible studies where they can learn from God's word.

When I became sober I wanted everyone to get sober because I experienced victory over a big struggle. When I became a Christian I wanted everyone to become a Christian because I experienced the joy and peace that comes from the salvation that Christ offers. Just because I had experienced the freedom that comes through surrender does not mean that others will change their lives in the same way. God has a plan for their lives. My role is to live with integrity because if I want to lead others, I need to be a good example.

I have a question for you: Have you ever tried to help someone? If so, take a moment to reflect on how it went or how it is going. What challenges have you experienced? Are you helping or enabling the other person? Have you seen evidence of change in the person's life? If so, don't stop. Keep going forward. If not, examine your role and approach to leading others. Spend some time in prayer for yourself and for the other person. Leading people can be challenging and sometimes discouraging but it can also be fruitful and rewarding.

One of the best ways I've found is by learning from my past successes and failures. When we help others to change their lives, it is important to remember that sometimes people can outwardly look like they are changing, but the real change comes from the inside out. Sometimes all you are seeing is an artificial change and not substantial change that will last. The Lord is the One who is able to truly see their heart and help them through their journey.

> *"For the Lord does not see as man sees; for man looks at the outward appearance, but the Lord looks at the heart."*
> 1 Samuel 16:7b, NKJV

God may put people in your life for you to help. Don't be afraid to teach others from your experiences. I think the biggest and most powerful gift we have is our testimony. A pastor friend once told me that "people don't care how much you know until they see how much you care." We must remember that some people are spiritually, mentally, or even physically unable to understand. Some of the people God places in your life may have never been able to trust anyone else before. In fact, you might be the first person they have ever met who is living a Christ-centered life. It is important to become their friend so that they can get to know you and build a trusting relationship. Leading others takes time and a commitment but I can tell you from my past experiences, it is well worth the effort.

Chapter 10

I Will...Not Enable Others

When is enough, enough?

E nabling is an obstacle which can really keep others from changing their lives. Often when you love someone, even though their life is a mess, it is difficult to make a decision to stop "helping" them. There is a fine line between helping and enabling someone.

I want to give you some suggestions that can help you and the person you love or are trying to help. I heard a pastor say, "The one who loves the most has the least control or power." I know from experience that this is true. Some of these suggestions might feel impossible, but you must remember that God loves the people in your life more than you can even think or imagine. You must believe this fact and not get discouraged because it is normal behavior for the addict or someone with a life-controlling habit to blame others.

Enabling is doing something for someone else who is capable of doing it for themselves. It is trying to fix someone else's problems when the responsibility is theirs to change. Enabling consists of making excuses, minimizing the situation and justifying for other's bad behaviors.

I remember my life was falling apart and I think everyone knew it but me. Years ago when I was in my addiction, I wanted to avoid phone calls, especially from customers or bill collectors. One day, I was in the kitchen and the phone rang. My wife answered the phone and said the call was for me. I told her, "Tell them I am not home because I am doing a job for someone." I did not want to talk to the person because I was working for them but I had not been showing up after they paid me some money. I was not being responsible and wanted to avoid the consequences of my negligence. During this time, my wife was changing and learning about enabling. So, instead of saying, "Ted isn't home," she told the customer, "Yes, Ted is home" and handed me the phone. I had no choice but to talk to the person.

You might think that my wife was being mean to me, but in reality, she was helping me. If she lied for me, then this would have enabled me to avoid being responsible. I can tell you this was the beginning of me knowing that my wife wasn't going to lie for me any longer. Lucetta decided not to be part of my problem and took a stand to not enable me any longer. I can tell you now this decision was hard for me and even harder for her.

It can be very difficult to know the difference between enabling and helping, especially when a loved one is involved. There are risks when we try to force or push someone to honestly look at their situation. They might not understand that you are trying to help them to deal with their issues, and this is where you might become a target of the problem in their mind.

It's helpful to know that you are only trying to help them get well. Those with life-controlling habits often have a unique way of blaming others for their problems. I encourage you to remember that you did not cause their problems and you are not the reason for their behaviors.

A challenge for you is to take some time and see if you are helping or enabling others. In some cases, we try to help and it seems like things are only getting worse. Most enablers do not want to acknowledge that they are playing a part in the person's lifestyle. Some of the excuses I have heard from enablers include: "They really are not that bad" or "they are home and not getting into trouble" (but nothing has really changed). This can be a dangerous situation because it not only affects you, but you are allowing the person to manipulate and continue their unacceptable behavior.

I encourage you to get some outside support because when someone is close to you, it is harder to make rational decisions because emotions tend to get in the way. This only adds confusion to the situation. Since this is very common, it is important to get help for yourself so that you can make wise decisions and stop enabling their negative behaviors. It is helpful to understand your part in the situation. I think it would be best to not let the person with the problem know that you are seeking help before you can take steps to stop the enabling behavior. They may notice that you are changing the way you interact with them but with support, you can continue to make the necessary changes in dealing with their problem. They may not like it, just like I did not like the changes my wife was making, but I can tell you that not enabling me was the most positive decision my wife made that helped both of us. I became more responsible and accountable for my actions which gave me a chance to start to actually deal with my issues and behaviors.

Chapter 11

I Will...Try the 30 Day Challenge

Can you teach old dogs new tricks?

I know from my experiences that training a dog when it is young is easier because the dog is more teachable. You can correct its bad actions before they become bad habits. In our home, my wife was usually the primary person to train our pets because I was running a business which often required working 10 hour days, 6 days a week. Even though she trained them, I was able to see that the older our dogs became, the more difficult it was to teach them new things. I believe this is the same for people as well.

Take a good look at your daily life. What is your routine? What happens to you when your routine changes or has an obstacle in it? How do you react in those unexpected situations? We often become so comfortable in our daily routines that it can limit our ability to be teachable.

So how does an adult learn to become like a child? Our mind has to be opened to different things. We need to believe despite not having all the answers. Therefore, don't be limited and stuck in your own thinking or ways. As you begin to change and learn new ways of living, you will develop a discernment to know what is right or wrong, be able to stop bad habits and begin good habits.

A habit can be defined as a routine part of your life and is a developed pattern of what you do. A habit may seem to be the only way someone can feel comfortable through their day. For example, some people cannot start their day without having a cup of coffee. Others cannot start their day without reading the Bible or praying for their concerns. Neither of these are bad habits, but their day does not feel complete without the normal routines.

For some people, a change in routine can cause a problem and lead them to have a bad attitude throughout their day. Sometimes people cannot function because their day has been different. Changing habits is not always easy and can also affect the lives of others. It is important to remember that we can always begin our day over and change our attitude at any time.

It has been said that habits are usually formed over 30 days. This means that if you do something every day for 30 days it will likely become a habit. So here is a challenge, find a habit in your life that you are having difficulty with giving up and try to resist that habit each day for 30 days. You can use the 30 day challenge for ending bad habits as well as starting positive ones. For example, in my life, I decided to start walking for 20 minutes each day, for 30 days. It has now been well over 30 days and I continue to make walking a regular part of my day.

We must remember that life is made up of different situations; therefore, try to let some things go for the moment. Remember that we can always make time for what's important.

Think on this for a moment: What habits are controlling you for the worse? Remember that doing something every day for a month leads to a new habit. What are some good habits you would like to develop in your life?

> *"Therefore, if anyone is in Christ, he is a new creation; old things have passed away; behold, all things have become new."*
> 2 Corinthians 5:17, NKJV

We are all a work in progress. I am 70 years old and there are still areas of my life what I am challenged in. Don't give up. You can do it!

Chapter 12

I Will...Help Others

Why me?

Remember that God has a plan for you. Most of the time, we do not know exactly what His plan is, but God wants us to prosper and is not out to harm you. Jeremiah 29:11 says, *"For I know the plans I have for you," declares the Lord, "plans to prosper you and not to harm you, plans to give you hope and a future."* God has plans for you and He will use you to help others if you let Him. For whatever you do or wherever you are, you can be used by God.

Sometimes God might use you just because you live or work in a certain place. For example, when I was working in construction, God gave me many opportunities to share my testimony with other workers. As a boss, God used me in how I handled situations and in my reactions to people. You may have opportunities to share your testimony or demonstrate Christ-like character while you are working at your place of employment.

As I look back, the most effective times I had an impact on someone's life occurred when I was not in a hurry, and I purposed to listen to them. I was willing to help the person in whatever situation they were going through. God orchestrates the times and places for these encounters. We never know when or where God will put people in our lives.

I remember recently I was asked to help at the Bridgeport Rescue Mission's Thanksgiving Food and Coat Drive where different stores provided food. Another man and I loaded the food on to the truck to be brought to the warehouse for its distribution. That was the extent of what I was asked to do, but God had another plan.

As we were coming back, I recognized a man who I knew from when I was growing up. He told me that he had stage 4 cancer and was going to die. He was very thin and looked like he weighed only 80 pounds. I told him we are all going to die one day. My biggest concern for him was when he dies, would he be in heaven or hell? So I asked him, and he didn't know. I explained to him that I know where I am going when I die. I realized that he did not want to hear me, but God was working in this moment because standing right behind me was his brother who had been listening to our conversation. After hearing me share some of God's Word, his brother wanted to pray and asked Jesus into his life. Moments like these are a part of God's plan.

When we are willing to help others, God will provide the people who need a relationship with Him. Take time and allow God to use you. Look for the opportunities God has for you. No matter what you do for a living, God wants to use you and wants you to share His

Good News with others. The best way to do this is to remember how God has given you a new day, so look at the victory you have in your life, and be willing to help someone. God does not see you as you see yourself. He looks at your heart. He uses us despite our feelings and shortcomings. God can use your past to help someone else change. I like the thought that we all can be used by God. So, why not you?

I believe to be effectively used by God, we need to have more of Him and less of ourselves. We need to put God first and shape our priorities to the things that matter most to Him. The best way to keep God first in our life is to read His Word, the Bible. Now don't get me wrong, this is not a cliché. For years, I heard that reading the Bible was important but when I actually started to spend time reading and studying His Word, I then understood why this was important. Studying God's Word has changed my life and has prepared me to help others.

Another way I try to put God first in my life is through spending time in prayer. Prayer is important for me because the outcomes or answers to prayer may be part of God's will for me. The best thing I could do for others is to pray for them and allow God to work in their life. This can be hard because emotions and feelings can get in my way. When helping someone, it is important to remember our role and responsibility in any situation. God is the One who is able to change others, and that is why it is important that we pray for others, especially those we are trying to help.

When you are asked the question, "Why me?", you will probably think many different answers to that question. God has made us all different and unique. There have been times when I would question God and I would ask Him, "Don't you think you could get someone better or more gifted than me to do what is in front of me?" Most of the time, I don't feel qualified to do what is asked of me. However I know that God uses the foolish things of this world to show His power and mercy. *1 Corinthians 1:27 says, "But God chose the foolish things of the world to shame the wise; God chose the weak things of the world to shame the strong."*

I remember when a pastor told me about someone in his church with a drinking problem. The pastor and some of the deacons met with this man to confront him about his problem. The man said, "I think I do have a drinking problem," but for whatever reason, he didn't want to attend any meetings or self-help groups that were non-Christian programs. The pastor learned about the Higher Ground Ministry and suggested this man should go to a meeting.

Surprisingly enough, the man said he would go. The meeting was on a Thursday night, and the only one who could take him was the pastor. I'm not sure, but I think the question he might have been asking himself was, "Why me?". The pastor knew that if there was any chance for this man to get some support, he would have to take him. The man came for about three weeks and then decided that he was going to move to Florida. As the pastor attended the meetings with his parishioner, he realized that he had a different problem in himself to address. He said that at the end of the day, he would go to the refrigerator like it was his best friend. He knew it was wrong, but he couldn't stop himself from binge eating.

The pastor originally went to the meeting in order to help another man. Yet, as he continued to attend the Higher Ground meetings, he surrendered his food binging over to the Lord. He knew food became an idol and an addiction in his life, but God gave him the victory. He was so blessed because of the change that happened in his life that he went to his church and asked permission to start a Higher Ground meeting there. The church agreed and he became very active in the Higher Ground Ministry and facilitated a meeting in his church for many years.

Just as this pastor was a blessing to the ministry and others, remember that you too can step out of your comfort zone and be a blessing to someone else. When you help others, you will find that you too receive a blessing.

Chapter 13

I Will...Care

Who cares anyways?

Have you ever asked yourself, "Who cares anyways?" I have asked myself this question many times. Sometimes I thought that no one cared about me. I felt this way because I didn't take the time to look at what I was doing. I didn't understand that I was living a very self-centered life.

As I think about some of the things I have done or said to people in order to get what I thought I needed, I really didn't care who I hurt. My life was always about looking for the next drug to make me feel better, and I had the nerve to believe that no one cared about me. Feeling like no one cares can seem like the truth to someone who is selfish because their thoughts are focused inwardly. When a person gets to this place in their life, it can become very real and can alter how they perceive the world.

My father was a gambler. If he was out of money, he knew how or who to borrow from. One day, I needed money so I went to one of my dad's friend's house. I had no right to do this because I am not my dad. My dad would borrow from him and pay him back. My intention was to use his money to get high and most likely never pay him back. Nevertheless, I went to his house and knocked on the door. He wasn't there, but his wife told me he was at the cemetery. I then went to the cemetery and found him there with a couple of men. Even though this man was at a cemetery paying his respects for a loved one, I didn't even question if it was okay for me to ask him for the money. I just knew he was my last resort so I went ahead and asked him if I could borrow some money. One of the men with him opened his coat as if he was packing a gun, but the guy with him said, "Leave him alone." I got in my car without the money and said to myself, "What is the matter with me?"

I was so desperate that I was willing to ask a man, who was well protected, for money so that I could get high. If I did not pay him back, it was possible that I would not see the next day. I felt so bad after this, but it still didn't stop me from my lifestyle of drugging. My life actually went from bad to worse.

When people get desperate, they tend to think that no one cares about them. What I have learned about being in a desperate state of mind is that I was the one who did not care about myself or others. If I did care about myself, I would not have let a drug control my life. Scripture teaches us how we can become a slave to sin. Jesus shares in John 8:34, *"Very truly I tell you, everyone who sins is a slave to sin."* When you feel like you have no one else to turn to and feel like you are alone, it is important to remember that this is selfish thinking.

When someone is in this state of mind, it's easy to believe that nobody cares about them, but it is not true. The problem is that many times, our friends or loved ones do not know how to really help. This is the choice you have to make if you care and want a better life. If other people do not seem to care about you, don't let that stop you from caring about yourself, and make the efforts to experience change.

Here is another example of what took place in my life. In 1968, I went to prison for the sale of heroin. I was arrested by the Federal Government, which took six months before I got arrested. I could not remember what I did after 6 hours or 6 days back then. Even though I was in trouble, I was lucky because this was my first drug offense. The Federal Government came out with a law called the Stamp Act for first time offenders. If you pleaded guilty, three years was taken off your sentence. Otherwise, it would be a mandatory five years. So I plead guilty and was out of jail in 14 months. Before I was released, my parents moved to another town, thinking that this would be better for me. When I was home from prison, it took me only 20 minutes to go to the same places I hung out before. Even though I was out of prison, my heart did not change, and I was still the same guy.

One night, I was coming home drunk and I do not remember if I cut this guy off or if he cut me off. All I know is that I pulled into our driveway, and he was at the end of the driveway. I grabbed a shovel and yelled for my brother and father to help. When my father got to the door, all he saw was me putting the shu. through the guy's windshield due to my anger. That night, my father had a heart attack and died.

I am telling you this to share what I did next. I had become such a hardened person that I don't think I had any feelings prior to this moment, but I remember crying at my dad's funeral. The sad part is that I kept living in my insanity for several more years. The only way for me to change was from the inside out. For me, that meant allowing God to change me since I was incapable of changing myself. I encourage you to give God a chance to change you for He has surely changed me.

It is a lie to believe that no one cares about you but if this is how you feel then I hope you can find hope in the Truth that God cares for you. 1 Peter 5:6-7 says, *"Humble yourselves, therefore, under God's mighty hand, that he may lift you up in due time. Cast all your anxiety on him because he cares for you."*

Chapter 14

I Will...Persevere

Do I get tired?

During the week, I am out many nights at different Higher Ground meetings. It is a blessing for me to be able to participate in these meetings. When others ask me if I get tired, my answer is usually "no". I can relate to the following Scriptures in God's Word.

> *"Do you not know? Have you not heard? The LORD is the everlasting God, the Creator of the ends of the earth. He will not grow tired or weary, and His understanding no one can fathom. He gives strength to the weary and increases the power of the weak. Even youths grow tired and weary, and young men stumble and fall; but those who hope in the LORD will renew their strength. They will soar on wings like eagles; they will run*

and not grow weary, they will walk and not be faint." Isaiah 40:28-31

I once heard my pastor say, "Christianity is not a solo sport." I like that because being a Christian and trying to do the right thing is not always easy. Many times, I have found growth in my walk when other Christians have helped me in whatever dilemma I was going through. I believe that to be a mature Christian I should be helping someone to get where I am spiritually and someone should be leading me in my walk with God to continue to grow stronger in my faith. I ask God for help in finding the right people to help me. Proverbs 27:17 says, *"As iron sharpens iron, so one person sharpens another."*

If you know someone who is not where you are spiritually, try to remember that only the grace of God got you where you are now. This will help you to be patient, and God will give you the strength you will need to have a positive effect in that person's life. There may be times when you have to ask someone who you trust to help you. In the Higher Ground Ministry Precept booklet, Pastor Tony Gibson explains that, *"The person we choose should be a mature believer, one who has been in the trenches, and has won some spiritual battles in his or her own life. One who is able to teach, exhort, rebuke, encourage and discipline and is willing to spend the time and assist us as we make the effort to change."* This is a healthy cycle of personal growth. You are being helped and encouraged in your walk with God, and you also are sharing with others to help and encourage them.

Jesus taught in John 15:12, *"My command is this: Love each other as I have loved you."* For me, that sounds pretty simple. All we need to do is love. However, at times this is more complicated than easy. It gets complicated when we love for our own satisfaction or when we are trying to get something out of others (like money, etc.). Wrong motives in love make it difficult because they are driven by selfishness. God did not intend for love to be self-centered but rather others-centered. He is our ultimate example of an others-centered love by what He did for us on Calvary. He loved us while we were sinners. Romans 5:8 says, *"But God demonstrates his own love for us in this: While we were still sinners, Christ died for us."* He did not wait until we were perfect to show us His love. We too need to have unconditional love for others.

I remember when I first got sober and my life started to get better, I bought my first new car. Shortly after, I received a phone call from my friend asking me to go with him to bring a man to detox. I went to meet my friend at his house. I didn't want to take my car because I did not know what condition this person was in and all I could think of was him throwing up in my new car. So, I parked my car and said that we could take my friend's car but he insisted that we would drive my car. My friend must have known what I was thinking, because he said, "It's just a car." I was taught a valuable lesson; my car is just a car and people are much more important that material items. It was the middle of winter, so when we got to the hospital, he was admitted. I took his clothes and went home. By the time I got home, my friend called me and told me that the man left the hospital. We couldn't understand how he got home and what clothes was he wearing! Nevertheless, I can't thank my friend enough for this lesson that I was taught.

When I was getting sober, I learned that when someone calls for help, it is important to go and try my best to see if I can help them. Those who call have different reasons for wanting help. They may be struggling with a problem and want advice. Or they may be calling me because they can't stop drinking or using drugs. Often, I asked them if they were ready for help and willing to stop. If they say "yes", I tell them I will bring them to the hospital to get detoxed. I also tell them if they stay, I will try to get them into a program. Some are not willing to go to detox. I share with them about the Higher Ground meetings and other support groups that may be able to help them. Others call me for accountability to help them stay clean and sober.

I have learned from experience, that many times people are at a place in their lives where they think they can stop their life-controlling habits by themselves. Once a person becomes addicted, there is a chemical need to get high. If I have the opportunity to meet a person like this, I ask them, "How has all of this been working for you?" If they tell me, "Not so good," I try to explain to them that their best thinking got them to where they are today. It is important to remember that in their minds they really believe that they can overcome their situations by themselves.

When helping someone I need to know my boundaries and that I cannot change others. I can tell them what helped me to change and bring them to meetings and church. People are not always ready or willing to receive what I am telling them and end up relapsing. The reality is that no one changes until they let God have His way in them. When I am concerned for a person and want to fix their problem, I may be getting in the way of God's plan. He wants to help this person and knows better than me what the person needs.

At times, serving in ministry and helping others can become demanding and tiresome. It can be physically, emotionally, and mentally draining but I continue to cling to God for strength. Galatians 6:9 says, *"Let us not become weary in doing good, for at the proper time we will reap a harvest if we do not give up."* There are many benefits to reap as we persevere, both in your life and in the lives of others.

Chapter 15

I Will...Look For the Impossible

Are you up to the challenge?

There is no way that I would be where I am today without God's help and grace. There is a saying that "God does not call the qualified, He qualifies the called." I am an example of this saying, and writing this book is proof that what seems impossible according to the qualifications given by the world's standards does not limit the ability for God to complete His calling of a task that He has set up for us. As taught in Luke 1:37, *"For nothing is impossible with God"* (NASB).

Usually an author of a book is very good at writing, but for me, writing this book is a task that I am not qualified for because reading and writing are not my strongest strengths. For years I had the desire to write a book in order to help others from the lessons I have learned in life. This is a desire that I believe God has given me and He is making it a reality despite my shortcomings.

Almost anyone can do what is possible; but to do the impossible takes faith. I know the impossible can be done with the help of the Holy Spirit. This is exciting for me to know that I am not doing the impossible by myself. God is helping me, and I have seen how He has provided others in order to help me accomplish this desire. I talked with my wife, and she encouraged me to start writing this book.

If you want to challenge yourself, try to do something you know you can't do, and then ask God to help you. I have been encouraged to see how God has been at work in my life during this time of depending on Him to strengthen my weaknesses in order to complete this task. God is not limited by our weaknesses, but He is glorified in using them in order to accomplish His will. In 2 Corinthians 12:9, Paul writes, *"But he said to me, "My grace is sufficient for you, for my power is made perfect in weakness. Therefore I will boast all the more gladly about my weaknesses, so that Christ's power may rest on me"* (NASB).

There have been many times that I have experienced discouragement in my life. For example, when I was getting off of drugs I began trying to be a good husband, father, and provider. While attempting to improve in these areas I became overcome with feelings of inadequacy. Even when writing this book, I have experienced these same feelings. Whenever I start to get discouraged and think that this is too big or impossible for me to do, God reminds me to not give up.

If you feel defeated and think, "I cannot do this," those thoughts are not from God, they are from the enemy. Satan wants to keep us bound in negative thoughts and especially keep us from doing something that would honor and please God. In John 10:10, Jesus tells us that, *"The thief comes only to steal and kill and destroy. I have come that they may have life and have it to the full."*

There are times when you may wonder, "Is this all there is in life?" or when feeling discouraged you might think, "Why try?" I encourage you when you feel down or insufficient, this is when it is critical to reach out to others for help. I have found this to be a very valuable lesson for myself.

During my career as a mason, I remember times when I would be asked to price a large job which I felt was way over my capability. However, the people that asked me to price their job believed that I was capable of doing the work. It was me who was feeling inadequate and incapable of doing this very big project. I would find someone who had experience in blueprint reading and pricing jobs to help me. Questions were asked of me such as how much work could get done on a good day and on a bad day. On a bad day, it is more difficult to get the work done if it is raining, and the work would have to be covered so the rain wouldn't affect the outcome of the job.

After receiving all the necessary information, I would quote a price for the project. Often I was called and asked if I could lower the price so that I could have the job. This is where I would have to make a decision to determine if the job was worth the price they were asking me to do the work for. Sometimes, I would accept a job and would try to learn from my decision. This is where the experience of trials and mistakes caused me to learn more as I overcame the doubts I was experiencing. In time, I became a very capable mason contractor with the experience to work on a variety of projects.

I remember being asked to price a job at Guenster Rehabilitation Center in Bridgeport. At one time, this building was a convent and had a chapel. The chapel was designed for the nuns to have quiet time with God. The director of the rehab, Bob, knew I was a Christian and brought me to the chapel. I was in the chapel for just a few minutes when Bob asked me a question which I will never forget. He said if I was in this drug rehab center and I was asked to go into the chapel for five or 10 minutes a day, "How would I feel?"

Now I put myself in the position of the people who may know about God and who may not know or care about Him. Some of them are forced to go into the rehab because they need to get better as they prepare to go to court. Others are trying to change their lives. I told him, "If I was asked to go to this chapel, it would be too overwhelming for me at that time in my life, and I probably would feel like I was going to hell." Then Bob asked me, "How can I change the atmosphere of the chapel to make it more inviting?" I told him if it was up to me. I would change it so that anyone who was going to the chapel would feel welcome.

The question he asked of me was, "What would I do to make it different?" I found the materials that would meet the desire Bob had in his mind which would not cause any structural damage to the building. He wanted me to put stone veneer on the inside of the walls. Back then, there was no thin stone for veneers so I was quite limited to what I could do. I remember he told me to do the best job I could do. So I started the job and emptied out the room and I remember that I ran into a problem. I went to his office and told him that there was a bench that I couldn't get outside of the room. I found out that whoever made this bench constructed it into pieces and put it together in the room.

When I told him what I discovered, he told me to cut it in half. I didn't know it at the time that he was asking me to do whatever was necessary to achieve the look and atmosphere that was to be created. He gave me this freedom, and my mind opened up to what this chapel could look like for anyone who was entering in to sit still and be alone with God. I didn't want the room to look overwhelming and wanted the presence of God to be in the chapel. There was a flat wall that was approximately 8' x 10'. I found a picture called "Come, Follow Me" which was made from mosaic ceramic tiles. The picture was a representation of Jesus with His arms reaching out.

On the floor, I installed a mosaic slate floor. Artificial stone was installed on the other walls. Two fountains with running water created a calm and serene atmosphere as the sound of water made the room very peaceful. I installed a bench all the way around the room which was made out of block and veneered with thin artificial stone and flagstone on top. I am telling you this because I had no idea of what it was going to look like, but I can tell you that many people have talked to me and others about this chapel and how it helped them look at God in a fresh and a new way.

For me, I was being asked to create a look with materials that would be structurally impossible for the room, but as I researched and found the appropriate materials, what seemed impossible became possible.

We can all learn from this experience because when there is a desire to accomplish a task or changing your life, there is always a way for it to be done.

BEFORE

AFTER

Chapter 16

I Will...Have Fun

Do you find it hard to have fun?

O ne time, I stopped at a bar for a drink, and I ended up staying for 14 years. Of course, I went home, but I thought I was having fun at the bar, hanging out with the guys and not facing life. Every night that I spent at the bar, I was not involved with my family at home. I was involved in bar fights and spent a lot of money that I did not have to spend. In my mind, I thought I was having fun but all I was left with was regrets. I kept getting high and then thought about how I could get my next drink or heroin fix. During this insane period of my life I was trying to escape from the problems that were in front of me. But these problems were only getting worse and so was I. This "fun" was really no fun at all.

Once I became clean and sober, I needed to find a new way of living. Fun did not come easily for me because I was too busy with work or not interested. I needed to come to the place of seeing that being a

Christian was not a list of rules but that with God in my life I was able to experience joy and contentment. Now there are many things that I enjoy doing which are fun.

As I continued to change, my life became full of many pleasurable activities. I was not afraid to try to do something I never did before. At age 40, I began snow skiing and taught my son and daughter how to ski. Due to double knee replacements in 2009, I do not feel comfortable skiing anymore. When I became 50, I learned how to golf and continue to play and enjoy golf very much. My wife learned to play golf also and now we are able to spend quality time together on the golf course. In our marriage, we serve God and like to spend time with each other. When our children were young, we made time for each other because we felt this was important to do in order to have a healthy marriage.

I enjoyed spending time with my family at Lakeside Christian Camp where we participated in many activities as a family. Through the years, we made many new relationships with other Christians. Lakeside was a place where we enjoyed relaxation as well as many activities and serving when help was needed. As a family, sometimes we would vacation in Stone Harbor at the New Jersey shore where we enjoyed the beach and riding the waves. This made me feel like a kid and it was something that I did not experience as a child. I was grateful for the ability to take my family on vacations. I worked very hard, and taking a week off was good for me.

Something I really enjoy doing is meeting new people. I find it to be exciting and fun. Others have described me as someone who is able to talk with anyone. I never looked at it that way, it is just something that I enjoy doing.

There are many other activities that I now find to be fun in my life, but in the beginning of recovery, changing how my time was spent was a little frightening. I had to deal with many different feelings and actually face my fears. This was an opportunity for me to grow and learn how to live a new life. In my early recovery, I learned that doing new things was important for me in order to move forward. Please remember to not let fear stop you from moving forward and being changed into a new person.

I am so grateful that I have a relationship with God because He has given me a purpose for living. He has changed the desires of my heart and delivered me from the bondage of alcohol and drugs. I desire to honor God and help others to know that there is a better way to live.

I encourage you to not be afraid of trying new healthy activities. For me, I enjoy golfing but for you it may be something else. There are many different sports, hobbies, and activities that you may enjoy. Like I said before, stick your neck out like the turtle and enjoy the gift you have been given. I have more fun now than I ever had in my life. We are here for only a short time so make the most of it. Thank you for taking time to read this book.

Your friend,
Ted

Chapter 17

Ted's Story

M y name is Ted and I was born in 1945 at Milford Hospital in Milford, Connecticut. One of my first memories is from when I lived in Shelton, Connecticut. My brother Victor and I were playing in the back-yard. Back then, we did not have garbage pickup, so my father used a 50 gallon barrel in order to burn our garbage inside it. But this day, while my brother and I were playing, we decided to try and burn the dog house. It caught on fire and we ran inside my father's barn, which was nearby. The fire got so big that the barn also caught on fire and we could not see or breathe. I grabbed my brother while trying to get out, but I lost his hand and I landed on the ground, trying to catch my breath. I ran for my mother, but it was too late. My brother died. Victor was four years old, and I was five.

I didn't know how I felt after this happened. I was confused and kept asking, "What happened?" I believe that my family thought that if they did not tell me the truth, then maybe I would forget about this incident.

But that was not true. I would try not to think about it, but when it came to my mind, I would ask again, and they would just tell me to "stop asking...it was not your fault." When I was around 35 years old, I asked my mother again. She started crying and said, "You were only five. I was the mother, I should have been watching." I think if they were honest with me, it could have helped to put some closure to the situation.

We later moved to Trumbull, Connecticut. I remember there was one red light, one policeman, one gas station, and a small store that had almost everything. My father was a drinker and a gambler; my mother gambled and played cards with her friends. I had an older sister named Gloria and a younger brother named Vinny. I can remember my mother trying to help us to learn how to read. She would get mad at us when we couldn't say the word correctly. When she became mad, I became fearful, which only made things worse. I would cry and then it would be my brothers' turn, and I would listen and laugh as he was getting yelled at.

In all fairness, my mother did the best she could, but when I went to school, I was filled with that same fear. I think this became part of me rebelling against learning. Learning lost its importance to me, so I had to learn how to survive. I found friends that did not care about school or learning either. When I was 16 years old, my father noticed that I was rebelling and not trying in school, and so he said to me, "You either go to high school or you get a job." So after two months of the 9th grade, I quit school. My father was a mason contractor, and for me, this seemed a lot easier than going to school. So I became a mason.

I have been arrested 23 times that I can remember. I was an alcoholic and a heroin addict. There were times that I drank cough medicine with codeine in it almost every day for about 3 years because it was sold over-the-counter and easy for me to get. I went to prison for selling heroin. I have been indicted for murder. I was shot in my mouth with a 38 pistol. The doctor said the only reason I lived was because I had a partial denture in my mouth which had turned the bullet. I lost eight teeth and broke my jaw. The bullet was in my neck and nine days later, the doctor removed the bullet. I then got strung out on morphine.

While I was in prison, my family moved to Stratford, Connecticut. I think they thought that if they moved, I would not get in trouble. But when I was released from prison, it did not matter that they moved towns because my heart did not change. One night, I was driving home drunk. I am not sure if I cut off a car or if they cut me off. I yelled for my brother and father, but because of my anger, by the time they got there, I had already put a shovel into the windshield of the other guy's car. That night, my father had a heart attack and died. He was 49 years old. I blamed myself for his death.

In 1969, I met my wife, Lucetta, at a local hotdog stand. I spent more time buying my first truck than marrying my wife. When we came back from our honeymoon, I began to use heroin again. We did not have a strong marriage. There were times that I would try to stop drinking and drugging but I kept on falling back to the substances. I tried the methadone program twice, but each time, I ended up drinking. My counselor from the methadone program told me that I needed to stop drinking if I wanted help. I knew that I was a drug addict, but I did not think I was an alcoholic. During this time, my wife went for help at Al-Anon. At these meetings, they told her to work on herself and that she was powerless over me. So she listened to their recommendation and began to work on herself. She became a Christian and God was working in her life. I remember one time I came home high and she saw the pain in me and gave me a hug rather than her former ways of fighting with me. I will never forget this moment.

During this time, I began to get grand mal seizures. It was at this point that I finally surrendered. I went to AA, and they helped me to stop drinking, but I knew I needed to do more than just stopping drinking. I needed to be changed from the inside out. I was one year sober when I became a Christian, and my life has never been the same. I have peace now and know that I am forgiven and free the bondage of drugs, alcohol, and destructive living. By God's grace, I have been sober and clean since September 10, 1977. I am a changed man. I am no longer a "me" person, now I am a "we" person. I desire to help other people find God and His son Jesus Christ.

My wife and I started a ministry called Higher Ground Ministry in 1988. It is a Christ-centered support group for helping addicts, family members, and those who struggle with any life-controlling problem. Higher Ground Ministry is a Christ-centered local church sponsored support group for anyone who has been personally affected by any addiction in their life or the life of a family member or friend. The foundation of this ministry is God's Holy Word which, alone, is sufficient to deal with addictive compulsive behaviors in our lives and the lives of others. We have found him and believe that the only way to be delivered is to have a relationship with God through His Son, Jesus Christ. This relationship is possible because of His atoning death on the cross and becomes a reality in our lives through repentance, faith, confession, and forgiveness. I encourage you to look at our website: www.highergroundministry.org.

This book is important to me because I know that it is not about how smart you are or how high your IQ is, but with the grace of God, surrendering your life, and willingness to change, victory is possible. I thought I would die as a drug addict or alcoholic, but God had a different plan. Every day is a gift from God. It is out of my comfort zone to write a book, but it is important to share what the Lord has taught me.

Make no mistake, education is highly important. My wife, Lucetta, finished high school and helped me with my business doing the office work. Our son, Tony, finished high school but always had a desire to learn the mason trade. He began working as a teenager and is now a successful mason contractor with his own business. He is married to Diane and has three daughters, Marissa, Adrianna, and Alisa. Diane helps Tony with the office work. Our daughter, Erica, has her master's degree in Occupational Therapy and is currently working and married to Raul who is an architect,

Spanish teacher and has a master's degree in public administration.

My life has had many high and low points but through it all I have come to experience the victory and deliverance that comes through surrendering to Jesus Christ. I am a new creation by His grace.

CPSIA information can be obtained
at www.ICGtesting.com
Printed in the USA
BVOW10s0342141117
500115BV00003B/3/P